Marine Mammals

ORCAS

ZELDA KING

PowerKiDS press

New York

Published in 2012 by The Rosen Publishing Group, Inc.
29 East 21st Street, New York, NY 10010

First Edition

Editor: Joanne Randolph
Book Design: Julio Gil

Photo Credits: Cover Tyson Mackay/All Canada Photos/Getty Images; pp. 4, 8, 17 © www.iStockphoto.com/Håkan Karlsson; pp. 5, 10 (bottom), 18, 19 Shutterstock.com; pp. 6 (top), 10 (top), 12, 22 © www.iStockphoto.com/Evgeniya Lazareva; p. 6 (bottom) Rick Price/Oxford Scientific/Getty Images; p. 7 Geo Atlas; p. 9 Jeff Foott/Discovery Channel Images/Getty Images; p. 11 Hemera/Thinkstock; p. 13 © Michael S. Nolan/age fotostock; pp. 14–15 Sylvain Cordier/The Image Bank/Getty Images; p. 16 Thomas Kitchin & Victoria Hurst/All Canada Photos/Getty Images; pp. 20–21 © www.iStockphoto.com/Chris Russick.

Library of Congress Cataloging-in-Publication Data

King, Zelda.
 Orcas / by Zelda King. — 1st ed.
    p. cm. — (Marine mammals)
Includes index.
 ISBN 978-1-4488-5335-9 (library binding) — ISBN 978-1-4488-5145-4 (pbk.) —
ISBN 978-1-4488-5146-1 (6-pack)
1. Killer whale—Juvenile literature. I. Title.
QL737.C432K56 2012
599.53'6—dc22

                                                    2011004923

Manufactured in the United States of America

CPSIA Compliance Information: Batch #WS11PK: For Further Information contact Rosen Publishing, New York, New York at 1-800-237-9932

CONTENTS

The Orca's Other Name 4

Where in the World Are Orcas? 6

What Makes Orcas Mammals? 8

Black and White and Shaped for the Sea... 10

All Sorts of Orcas.. 12

Wolves of the Sea 14

The Ways of the Orca.. 16

A Place in the Pod 18

Growing Up 20

Orcas and People.. 22

Glossary... 23

Index 24

Web Sites.. 24

The Orca's Other Name

What kind of whale is not a whale? The killer whale, or orca, is really a large dolphin. It is easy to see why people might think it is a whale, though. Like whales, orcas are large **marine** animals. They are about 30 feet (9 m) long and weigh about 20,000 pounds (9,000 kg). That is almost the size of a school bus!

How did orcas get the name killer whales? Long ago, sailors saw orcas kill huge whales and so called them whale killers

Orcas are mostly black on top, which makes them hard to see from above. Their light-colored undersides make them blend in from below, too.

or killers of whales. Over time, the name changed into killer whales, even though these animals were not whales themselves.

Orcas have white patches near their eyes, behind the fins on their backs, and on their sides. The fin on an orca's back can be almost 6 feet (2 m) tall!

Where in the World Are Orcas?

Would you like to see orcas? You can do that in many places. Orcas live in all the world's oceans. People are the only **mammals** that live over a larger area. Orcas favor cold water, like that found in the Arctic Ocean and Antarctic Regions. However, some live in warmer water. Most orcas live in coastal waters. They are often seen off the west

Above: This group, or pod, of orcas is swimming off the coast of British Columbia, in Canada, just north of Seattle, Washington. *Right*: These two orcas have popped above the ice in Antarctica to look for seals.

Where Orcas Live

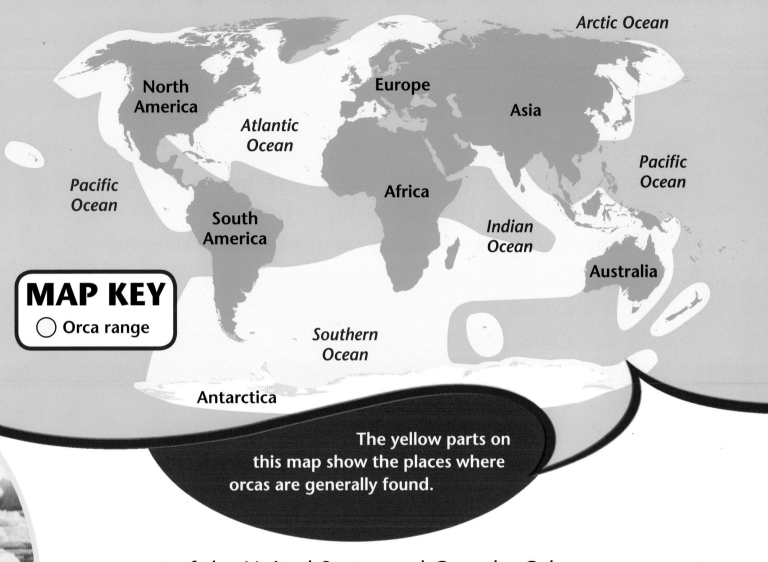

North America

Europe

Asia

Arctic Ocean

Atlantic Ocean

Pacific Ocean

Pacific Ocean

Africa

South America

Indian Ocean

Australia

MAP KEY
○ Orca range

Southern Ocean

Antarctica

The yellow parts on this map show the places where orcas are generally found.

coast of the United States and Canada. Other orcas live in the deep ocean far from land.

You can also see orcas in aquariums and marine parks. Orcas are smart, and people enjoy watching them in shows.

What Makes Orcas Mammals?

Orcas look like fish. What makes them mammals then? Orcas are **warm-blooded** and have backbones, just as all mammals do. They breathe air, too. Orcas must hold their breath underwater and come to the top of the water to breathe.

Like other mammals, female orcas give birth to live calves, or babies. They drink milk from their mothers' bodies for at least a year.

You might be wondering about one other thing, though. Mammals have hair or fur. Orcas do not have either. Calves do

Orcas breathe through blowholes on top of their heads. When they are underwater, folds of skin tightly seal the blowholes to keep water out.

have hair while they are inside their mothers' bodies. They lose it before they are born. That is because having smooth skin helps orcas swim faster.

Like most mammals, orca mothers care for their young for a period of time after they are born. Here a mother and calf orca come up to take a breath together.

Black and White and Shaped for the Sea

You likely know what orcas look like. They are easy to recognize because of their bold black-and-white coloring. Orcas are black on top and white on the bottom. They have white spots near each eye, called eye patches. They have another white spot on each side near their tails. They also have gray areas, called saddle patches, behind their **dorsal** fins.

Above: Orcas have powerful tails. The parts at the end of their tails are called flukes. *Right*: Here you can see the white eye patch on this orca. You can also see the white underside of this large marine mammal.

Each orca has markings that are a bit different from those of its fellow orcas. Scientists use these markings to help tell orcas apart.

Orcas are shaped for swimming. Their long, rounded, smooth bodies get narrower at each end. Orcas have paddle-shaped **flippers** to guide them through the water. Their tall dorsal fins help keep them steady as they swim.

All Sorts of Orcas

Did you know that different groups of orcas look different? These groups have different ways of life, too. In the northern Pacific Ocean, **resident** orcas have rounded dorsal fins, live near shore, and eat fish. **Transient** orcas have pointed dorsal fins, move around a lot, and eat marine mammals. Offshore orcas are smaller than the others and eat fish.

All male orcas have tall dorsal fins that are shaped like triangles. Females have smaller dorsal fins that generally curve backward.

This orca is part of a group of more than 25 Type C orcas that was hunting near Paradise Bay in Antarctica.

In the Antarctic Regions, Type A orcas have no saddle patch, live offshore, and eat small whales. Type B orcas have large eye patches, live near shore, and eat seals. Type C orcas have small eye patches, live near shore, and eat fish.

Wolves of the Sea

Orcas are sometimes called wolves of the sea. Can you guess why? It is because they often hunt in packs, as wolves do! A pod of orcas circles its **prey**, then attacks.

Orcas are built for hunting. Their large mouths have 40 to 56 sharp teeth. These teeth are about 4 inches (10 cm) long! To find prey underwater, orcas use **echolocation**. Some have special methods for catching prey that is on land or ice. They make waves to wash seals off floating ice. Sometimes orcas leave the water and slide onto beaches to catch seals or penguins!

Did You Know?

Some surprising types of prey have been found in the stomachs of dead orcas. Among the animals these orcas have eaten are sea turtles, polar bears, and even moose!

This sea lion may have thought it was safe on the beach. An orca rode a wave right up onto the beach to catch it, though. The orca will then slide back into the water to eat its prey.

The Ways of the Orca

Have you ever seen a whale jump out of the water, then land with a huge splash? Orcas enjoy **breaching**, too, and it is an amazing sight.

Another orca **behavior** is **spy hopping**. Can you guess what it is? It is when orcas pop their heads above the water to look around. Orcas also like to slap the water with their tails and flippers.

Why do orcas do these things? We are not sure. Spy hopping likely helps

This orca is breaching. Breaching orcas generally land on their sides or their backs.

orcas spot prey on land or ice. It may be a way of playing, too. All these behaviors may be play for these smart animals.

Here an orca is shown spy hopping. Its powerful tail helps it hold its head out of the water.

A Place in the Pod

Orcas are social animals. They like to be with other orcas. They live in groups, called pods. A pod can have from just 2 or 3 orcas to 50 or more.

Among some animals, males are the group leaders. However, females are the bosses in orca pods. Pods commonly form around one or two females and their children.

Pod members talk to each other using a language of squeals, squawks, and screams. All orcas

Orca pods generally have the females and young in the center. Males are toward the outside of the group.

make these sounds. Each pod has its own special language, though. Even from far away, an orca can recognize the language of its pod.

Two or more orca pods may sometimes come together for a while. Scientists call these groupings herds.

Which do you think is bigger, a baby orca or you? Newborn orcas are about 8.5 feet (3 m) long and weigh about 310 pounds (140 kg). That is much bigger than even grown-up people are!

Babies are born tail first underwater. Their mothers take very good care of them. As they grow, calves learn how to hunt and speak the pod's language. Some types of orcas spend their whole lives in the same pods. Among other types, young orcas leave when their mothers have another baby.

Orcas start to have babies in their teens. Females have one baby every three to five years. Orcas live 30 to 80 years!

Female orcas carry their babies inside their bodies for about 17 months before giving birth. Then the mother and baby stay close to each other for many months.

Orcas and People

The orca's other name, killer whale, makes it sound scary. However, there are no known cases of wild orcas hurting people. In fact, there are stories of wild orcas guarding people from sharks!

Even though orcas are not generally a danger to people, people are a danger to orcas. **Pollution** produced by people is in the oceans and in orcas' prey. Hunting and fishing by people have also cut down the supply of prey for orcas. Boating can hurt orcas, too.

Orcas have not yet become **endangered**. If we take care of these wonderful animals now, maybe they never will be.

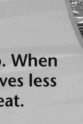

People eat fish, just as some orcas do. When people overfish in some places, it leaves less food for animals such as the orca to eat.

GLOSSARY

behavior (bee-HAY-vyur) Ways to act.

breaching (BREECH-ing) Jumping out of the water.

dorsal (DOR-sul) Positioned on the back.

echolocation (eh-koh-loh-KAY-shun) A method of finding objects by producing a sound and judging the time it takes the echo to return and the direction from which it returns.

endangered (in-DAYN-jerd) In danger of no longer existing.

flippers (FLIH-perz) Broad, flat body parts that help animals swim.

mammals (MA-mulz) Warm-blooded animals that have backbones and hair, breathe air, and feed milk to their young.

marine (muh-REEN) Having to do with the sea.

pollution (puh-LOO-shun) Man-made waste that harms Earth's air, land, or water.

prey (PRAY) An animal that is hunted by another animal for food.

resident (REH-zuh-dent) Having a small home range and always returning to the same places.

spy hopping (SPY HOP-ing) The act by an orca of getting its body in an up-and-down position and sticking its head above the water.

transient (TRANT-shee-ent) Having a larger home range than resident orcas and moving around in ways that cannot be guessed in advance.

warm-blooded (WORM-bluh-did) Having a body heat that stays the same, no matter how warm or cold the surroundings are.

INDEX

A
aquariums, 7

B
backbones, 8
behavior(s), 16–17
breaching, 16

C
calves, 8, 20

D
dolphin, 4
dorsal fins, 10–12

E
echolocation, 14

F
fish, 8, 12–13
flippers, 11, 16

K
killers, 4–5
kind, 4

L
language, 18–20

O
ocean(s), 6–7, 12, 22

P
Pacific Ocean, 12
patch(es), 10, 13

P
people, 4, 6–7, 20, 22
pod(s), 14, 18–20
pollution, 22
prey, 14, 17, 22

S
sailors, 4
school bus, 4
size, 4
spy hopping, 16

T
teeth, 14

W
water(s), 6, 8, 11, 14, 16
whale(s), 4–5, 13, 16, 22

WEB SITES

Due to the changing nature of Internet links, PowerKids Press has developed an online list of Web sites related to the subject of this book. This site is updated regularly. Please use this link to access the list:

www.powerkidslinks.com/marm/orcas/